MW00427015

tracings of your hand every year

This Book Belongs To

Recorded By

how we celebrated your birthday

a drawing of you

favorite walks and parks

tea parties and box trains

flowers you pick

visiting relatives

our nighttime rituals

wagon rides

the piles you make
and how you organize your world

new words and capabilities

your stories of what happened
before you knew how to speak

animals you love

18

gardens you plant

best places to hide

treasures found and saved

ADVENTURES AND TRAVELS
explored this year

BOOKS READ THIS YEAR

HOLIDAYS AND RITUALS
celebrated this year

DREAMS AND WISHES
for the next year

how we celebrated your birthday

forts we build and
imaginary worlds we make

a drawing of you

who you pretend to be—
animals and characters in favorite books

what we do at the park

what you pack for adventures

HOW YOU ARE BIG

how you are little

where you keep special treasures

bath-time fun

how you fall asleep

how you wake to the new day

the tallest tower ever built

plans made

favorite foods to forage

favorite foods to eat

.

how you are cared for by others

your friends

ADVENTURES AND TRAVELS
explored this year

BOOKS READS THIS YEAR

HOLIDAYS AND RITUALS
celebrated this year

DREAMS AND WISHES
for the next year

how we celebrated your birthday

the stories you share

a drawing of you

favorite dance moves and costumes

nighttime rituals and dreams

how you solve problems

how you find calm

your friends
and the games you play together

your jokes
and what is silliest to you

writing your name and other new skills

what you do outside

what you do inside

what frustrates you
and how you figure out solutions

how you show love

what you focus on best

ADVENTURES AND TRAVELS
explored this year

BOOKS READ THIS YEAR

DREAMS AND WISHES
for the next year

how we celebrated your birthday

a drawing of your family and home

a drawing of you

challenges and adventures in learning

your teachers

your favorite library sections

old friends and new friends

the games you play

your growing body and mind

interests and passions

how you help

the work you do

what you are excited to learn about

your favorite places around town

the worlds you imagine

world events

world discoveries

ADVENTURES AND TRAVELS
explored this year

HOLIDAYS AND RITUALS
celebrated this year

DREAMS AND WISHES
for the next year

how we celebrated your birthday

your first tooth!

a drawing of you smiling

night adventures and wishes on stars

your growing strength and new capabilities

the things you do

special objects you make

bike riding and skinned knees

your teachers

learning even more

the jokes and stories you share

kindness to friends

adventures with friends

explorations of the big world

favorite games and sports

what you like to draw

your dream day

ADVENTURES AND TRAVELS
explored this year

BOOKS READ THIS YEAR

HOLIDAYS AND RITUALS
celebrated this year

DREAMS AND WISHES
for the next year

family histories and
stories from your elders

the lives they led,
their work, and their loves

letters to you

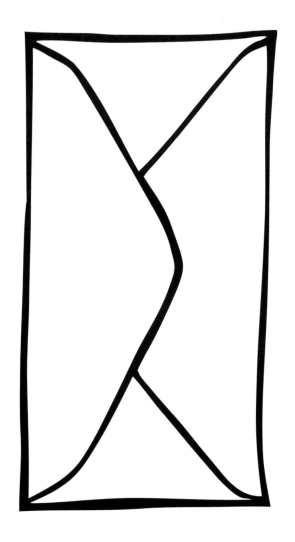

About The Author

Nikki McClure uses an X-Acto knife to create intricate, beautiful paper cuts from a single sheet of paper. Her evocative language translates the complex poetry of motherhood, nature, and activism into a simple and endearing picture. Her art can be found in her annual calendar, notecards, journals, and children's books. She lives in Olympia, WA.
www.nikkimcclure.com

Printed in China

Published by Sasquatch Books
20 19 18 17   9 8 7 6 5 4 3 2

Editor: Susan Roxborough
Project editor: Em Gale
Design: Joyce Hwang

Library of Congress Cataloging-in-Publication Data is available.

ISBN-13: 978-157061-943-4

Sasquatch Books | 1904 Third Avenue, Suite 710 | Seattle, WA 98101
206.467.4300 | www.sasquatchbooks.com | custserv@sasquatchbooks.com